THE GREATER PURPOSE
Book Three: The Purpose Trilogy

Enact Your PURPOSE

then ...
Reach for the Stars

Robyn G. Locke

GIVEN BY THE ELDERS

Golden Page
PUBLISHING

Table of Contents

In Appreciation

Words are hard to express when all you feel is gratitude for what has been given in unconditional and unending Love. I am so grateful to the Elders who impart their insights when I have sought alignment and am receptive to receive. I hope you are open and ready to receive what is being given here in the Light and Love in which it is shared.

I extend my gratitude to Kate, who enabled my Greek adventure to become tangible and real. She made it all possible, from arranging a fantastic writer's retreat to assisting with its many distinctive nuances. From start to finish, Kate was in the midst of it all. What an incredible time and journey, with the beautiful Greek Islands as the backdrop. Thank you to each who played a role in this stunning trek. I hope workshop participants continue to see new perspectives as they delve more deeply into the boundless teachings and knowledge imparted by the Elders.

A big thank you to Lorie, Victoria, Lorna, and John for making this book and audiobook possible.

Might you be in that space of Loving embrace, acceptance, and allowing as you consider your own unique journey. Maybe use this book as a springboard for your customized adventure. Allow purposeful realizations to bubble up and resurface as you seek to enact and discover more.

Introductory Prologue

In the beauty of the day, will you awaken to what is around you … that which is real and that which is for your experience here? Will you look upon life with the wonderment and awe of which it is truly conspiring and inspiring within the pathway that you traverse? As All* does seek entrance into your knowingness to reach you beyond the mental aspect that does engage and enlist you to do this or that in a meaningful or not way.

*All refers to its singular use and understanding for all are the one.

And so we would say this day, might you look upon all that are the wonders of the day. All that do greet you and do express themselves to you so you see the wonderment which is all around you waiting to be exposed, as it is composed of all the things that will bring you into that space of another know-ingness … another pathway of purpose … another aspect of being … another way to perceive and receive life so that you might not feel downtrodden and weary from your travels here.

For your journey in many ways has just begun because in this evoking of wanting, and knowing, and seeking, you then embrace all that might be in a different way. For you embrace a perspective unlike any other. You embrace that which is an expression of who you are and who you are meant to be as you traverse in this journey known as life.

And so seek this day to move in the way of wonderment for all that might be enlisted. So that each day that progresses from this one is more carefree, is more light-hearted, is more in keeping to move you to that purposeful direction which you so sought when you entered into the rounds of incarnation here.

For when you knowingly move in a manner that does progress you in a different way than perhaps before, you now see things and life within your midst differently … do you see? You recognize the gifts given even in the negativity you once thought they evoked. You look at the colors and the fragrances, and the aspects of taste and feel and that knowing, and you recognize that it is felt differently than before.

It is felt for experiential purposes and nothing more. You do not engage in the dramas of the day. You do not enlist in the dramas that present themselves, but you chuckle at their merriment and worth … with mirth.

For you see, all elicits for you to engage from the Conscious Awareness from that which does rest within you and does await engagement, and does seek to express itself so that you might enlist in the beauty of the day in a different way.

Enlist in the beauty of the day in a way in which you may not have engaged with that beauty and light before. Then you see life and things differently, do you see? And in that contemplative moment, in that meditative stirring of activity that is not from the mind, but from, perhaps, your heart center, that then you look upon life and do recognize that this body vessel, this Spiritual Form known as your Soul, and Source Energy have all aligned and conspired to gift you this experience.

And so we say embrace this and all life. Embrace that which is the wonderment of which it is. Embrace to know, to be in that space so that all might become known to you. So then you move in a more purposeful and aligned way — to receive and be perceived as that one of knowingness. So that then others move to emulate what you do. They do this and not that. They see the light and the mantel that you carry, for you move throughout this life in a more purposeful direction and way.

And that is what we seek throughout the gifts offered within this telling, within this book, and its pages. For as you read here, know that all is as it might be for your interpretation and the perspective that you hold. For each is that gift. Each is that gift to be perceived and received in the time that you are accessible to its understandings and the value of what is given. For you see, if you move in the manner that you have moved in previously, you perhaps have missed some of the beauty and light which does unfold around you.

And as you recognize that these things are all gifts given so that you choose the path that is most preferred, so that you get about the business of why you incarnated here originally — why you chose that original incarnation to move into form, to feel and perceive that which was unknown from a spiritual vantage point — that which was unknown and yet wanting to be experienced and recognized ... *experienced and recognized.*

Recognize and move in the manner that will gift you what you seek to experientially know and then enlist life from that vantage as you move about. Offer gratitude, and in that space of gratitude, do elicit those things that you have recently discovered. Elicit those things so that then they go out to Universe, are multiplied, and returned back to you as you know.

For many times it is not the knowing, but it is the doing that is amiss and missing from the landscape of your life ... for you have gathered much knowledge. You have gathered and tucked it away ever so safely so it is accessible when you are ready to engage and move in that manner.

But we say, do not put off what you might

do today. For there is opportunity in this and each day moving forward as you progress in this life. There is opportunity. And there is that which is what we would say wonderment and allowing, as there is that entrance into this world of form.

And so see life as fluid and flowing. See life as ever-changing … expanding, and contracting based upon your actions and efforts — based upon what you seek to know — based upon what you seek to find — based upon what you look to engage with … this day.

Enlist this day with Love. Begin this day in Love and call Universal Love into the platform of your daily awareness. Express It. Move It out into the world of form. Express this Love and the wonderment that It is. And in so doing, more will return back to you.

More will be in that space for you to be in the space of Loving embrace. And then your days will be fuller, and you will move back into the world of form that which is a necessary and needed component.

For you see, all life is healed and made whole through the energy of Universal Love and Its engagement in this day.

I received the Introductory Prologue and the first five chapters of this book, Enact Your Purpose, *in Lesvos, Greece. Might you be receptive to receiving this gift of Love? Undertake to embrace their measures, words, and these pages so all might evoke a remembering as you step through the veil to know more of what is yet to be.*

How to Receive to Perceive

This book will enable an inner discovery and personal transformation to occur. Might you begin your engagement here when you are ready to be in that contemplative or meditative sort of way? Engage by enlisting one of our many meditations to set the mood. This will enable you to enjoy a frequency adjustment. This adjustment is the best means for a receptivity to occur and for our insights to be more readily perceived and received.

As we move forward in Light and Love, know that all is a matter of acceptance when it is time for you to do so. Might you be in that space now? Be in that space where the mental box does not reside, and there is an allowing of all that is to progress this day.

Having placed the mental box upon the shelf — locked it, blocked it, we now seek to allow more to move into that mental space that was once occupied by something with a sheer knowingness. But today, there is that opportunity for more. And so enlist and move this day to absorb, and expand, and calibrate, and be all that you were intended to be in this lifetime, as you embrace more. And so, we move to discuss something of deep importance and something that …

We do want you to know
That all is in the mix of flow.
When you are reverent and willing to know
What more might be awaiting and bestowed.

For now through Light and Love we do progress
To give to you all that we now profess.
And it is in this measure that we describe
That all is given in Love,
For it is in Love where we do reside.

Let us travel this road of discovery together as we embark and provide how each tomorrow might become more effortless. In this way, each new day will seek to reveal more of what you desire to be made tangible and real.

Now you will have the means to enact and bring
about all you seek to come … into being.

Given by the Elders

Chapter 1

Awaiting Focus

As we consider the best starting point for these discussions and all that is to move forward, we ask you to center your focus and to be in that space of Loving embrace. That you might know, and be inclined to know, something that has been lost perhaps in time but is still accessible through these messages, recordings, insightful gifts.

And so, do embrace each thing moving forward. Embrace each as you move to adopt and adapt to insights gleaned as you seek more. Might we move this day to be in that oneness, so that you might express and illuminate those offerings in a most expedient and Loving way?

Might You Sharpen Your Focus Now

Might you consider moving in the manner that does not restrict the flow and all that might be imparted this day? We seek to give you Loving insights and those things which will propel your steps forward in a most expedient way.

You see, we center and focus upon that which you seek and which you sought before coming into human form. But because of the densities that are in play and in place, and all that exists within the physicality of this life experience, do you see that many components that were unseen were lost over time and over the many incarnations that perhaps the one or the other has experienced? And so know that although time does not exist here as it does there, that there is a need in this time, to consider moving and stepping up what has existed before so that you do not continue in the rounds of incarnation on this Earth platform.

And so we have come, and there are many who have traveled and tarried here so that this objective might be realized … for there are those who have been lost here for a time and believe that the dramas within the day are those things which are necessary for them to engage in. And by this, we mean that those who had once sought or wanted to achieve certain objectives and understandings that they then have the opportunity to return to why they embodied in the first place.

But when various activities or undertakings are seen as a need to correct, a need to engage with to perhaps change the flow in which they currently exist, so that truth does prevail. So that honor does prevail. So that justice does prevail. Then they turn away from that which they might ordinarily seek to know, to right that wrong.

And we will tell you that within each lifetime, there have been those things which have drawn one or the other into an activity that is all-consuming. And the rightness of a wrong is a just thing. And bringing justice to an unjust situation is a good thing. And so we do not say that one supersedes the other, but rather, might you consider that now is the time to move about this life so that you might enact why you came here and what you set up into motion in doing so.

We will share, as discussed in *The Original Purpose* book, that when you moved into that in-between state, oftentimes, although you believed you know all, that this is not so. That at this point, you know as you knew on Earth when you were physically placed. And so, although you may believe you are right, and just, and deser*ved* of the understanding you now hold, and the belief you hold — that those may be as they were gleaned on this Earth platform.

In other words, you carry with you that

understanding. You carry with you the understandings that you held while physically placed. And so, although you are given reinforcement, you then do not move from a more enlightened space. And it is then that you carve out your next life experience, and it is using faulty material. It is using not complete information. It is done using that information which you currently believed while in embodiment.

So there is not the stepping up perhaps, although this is not always the case. But there is often not the full totality of understanding that would allow that next embodiment to be more enlightened and moving forward from a more aligned space.

This is the methodology, and the purpose of these books. It is to give you more for consideration and contemplation. And as always, we advise that you seek a centeredness and a moving within to determine if these teachings are right for you. And if they will expand what you currently know as these understandings cause what you understand to grow.

And so this day, as we begin this next chapter of your life, as you weave it into the considerations that exist within your being and world, might you know that all moves in this way in Love, for we are the energy of Love. And we seek for you to anchor and be in the space where Loving embrace can be accepted, acknowledged, and incorporated into your day moving forward in a most Loving way.

For all does move as the ebb and flow of the ocean or the seas that surround, for there is a Loving, wafting energy that does become immersed and incorporated within the dynamic of the one who does seek engagement there.

So know that this Earth does offer many beautiful and wondrous opportunities to still the mind. To still the racing contemplations that the mind actually throws into the path of the one who is, what we would call, a seeker.

Know that the many checklists, the many objectives that the mind and especially egoic mind do produce within one's day … that they are all not necessary. And that in the doings that are suggested and proposed, as you move about, are actually distractions that keep you from moving in a most and more expedient way to the path of your enlightenment.

You see, you came to understand an

energy. You came to understand an energy that we will call your purpose or mission for being in this life. And that purpose or mission is unique unto you. You set out a platform; you set out an objective; you set out something that you wished to undertake and know more fully. And in doing so, you must also experience its converse energy. For it is in the converse, or the opposite (opposing) energy, that you discover the full totality of that which you wish to know.

Many individuals that chose to embody in the delicate nature of their Soul Essence, and not having experienced the densities of the Earth platform in previous times, did quite literally get taken out of embodiment when their converse energy, or that opposing energy, introduced itself into their life path. For it was a shock, oftentimes, to experience that which was not in alignment with what was sought.

Without having a clear understanding of what they were stepping into, the Soul Essence, in its naivety of what was to befall them, did not know how to react or how to take in what was being given. And perhaps, let us say, they did not perceive or receive what was given as a gift. They do not look upon it in the whimsical wonderment that it was.

And so often in this way, many lifestreams did pass from the physical platform into that in-between time. And it is there that the strategizing, and the planning, and putting forth of the next life path does take place. But you see within the undertakings of the original purpose in that original lifetime, there is not the full awareness, moving forward, of that which they knew before because the understanding of where they came from, and what their objective was, was now a bit masked.

And they did not remember what they had set out and put into play. And they did not remember their divine heritage. They remembered components of the life from which they had just passed. And we will say too that beliefs are carried with the one, into this next phase. And so, although there is not the full recall, there is the general understanding of what might be and what is wanted. But it is from a more fragmented formation. In other words, there is not the totality of understanding or recall.

There are components that are recalled, and there are delineations of what was in occurrence in that lifetime. But it is almost, we would say, the big picture of the life experience that is photographically recalled and given (but) in a most Loving way, but without the mind or ego inserting during this time.

But you see, the structuring and the moving from the lifestream, from physicality to this in-between time and then back into embodiment, does not have all of the parameters and all the components that it once knew before physically embodying the first time. In other words, there is not the totality of understanding that was given and held by the Soul Essence upon that initial embodiment.

And so as embodiments occur successively, there is less and less of a recall of the objective that was sought. And so now you have many lifestreams that have been incarnating for many, many, many rounds of embodiment. And we would say there are those who believe that this is all there is. And we will say this is as it is for a purpose, but it has lost some of the core and intrinsic components that would allow the one to reconnect to their original mission and their original purpose for incarnation.

And we have sought and do now seek for that reconnection to be further anchored and recognized. And so we have given books, and blog posts, and teachings that will allow the one to have the opportunity for that insight to bubble up to the surface … to bubble up and to be known. For oftentimes, the mind does confound for it cannot understand much beyond its own measure. And so these more lofty undertakings are not within its realm of consideration.

And so perhaps your mind does wander — perhaps your mind does fixate and focus upon one thing and not another. And so you miss valid considerations that are no longer a part of the dynamic because you quite frankly do not hear them. Or you resonate with something that does sound familiar, but you miss the newer components that are given that might help you strategize as you move about this life to choose and make better choices. Or those choices which will move you in the direction preferred. For we will say that there is no good or bad choice, for each will move you in the direction which you seek for that expansiveness and that directive to be embraced.

So now let us say that as you seek to know, and as you seek to align into the oneness of All that is, might you do so from the posture of Love and Loving embrace? Of knowing that these things are given so that you might better navigate this life moving forward … so that you might better navigate all you seek to know. So that at the conclusion of this life, you might no longer incarnate into this Earth platform but move in a manner free from the constrictions and the requirements of embodiment.

There is the need prior to departing here to bring wholeness and completion to the Soul Essence, which may have been coming here for quite a time. For you see, there are those different things that do occur that splinter a Soul. And so always seek to move, and to regroup, and regain, that which was lost in time and over time.

When regaining and joining together

those components that were fractured or splintered away from the Spiritual Essence, then there is the totality of the Whole that does then have the opportunity to reclaim all components of Itself or of Its Being.

And so always seek wholeness in each regard … wholeness to bring that clarity so that there is not that fractured state when moving from this (physical) plane to another.

⧈ Enlist The Following Instruction Contemplatively or Meditatively ⧈

And so now we seek that centeredness. And we ask for you to place (your) feet firmly upon the floor with your hands in a manner that will allow for energy to effortlessly and effectively move throughout your being and form. We ask for you to see light swirling about as it comes from all directions above you, entering into the vessel that you know as your personality or self.

See it fully embrace each cell, organ, and body part so that there is a light energy that does infuse and flow throughout you. Now see that light traveling from your form, down through your feet, and down into the center of the Earth.

Now see a swirling, and an anchoring, and a Loving embrace that comes from the energetic flow of that substrata of Earth as it moves to embrace you. Then, feel each moving out to fully encircle and anchor you into the form in which you now reside.

The energy then travels back from that anchoring position and posture into the body form, giving you the anchoring of this Earth platform as you move about the day, so you do not flit and float throughout the process of your undertakings.

See light energy infuse and engulf you now. See light energy sparkle and be that effervescent light that does permeate and saturate your form. Feel a renewal as Love anchors you into the physicality of your existence now. And know that Loving support and guidance is with you always.

Call to those who reinforce your lifestream in prayer, in meditation, in contemplation, and in all activities as you seek to know more — for there are those who travel with you concurrent to each embodiment that are there to answer your calls and questions. They have an energetic connection to you. And in that energetic connection, you can hear, and see, and know their responses. Perhaps not to physically see them but to see signs that you determine and establish along the way.

And so as these signs, and platforms, and understandings are embraced, and you do recognize them as being gifts to know which way to go when you do move in a more enlightened and, might we say, inspired way. Always seeking and asking to know that path which will propel you in the right direction for you to accomplish all you seek to know.

For you see, this is the yearning. This is the wanting. This is the determination that you have sought, and that is perhaps amiss in this lifetime now. For when there is a lack of fulfillment — when there is a hole, let us say, within your world that does not seem to be filled and infused, as it might be, it is because there is a lacking of that which is sought and was sought in another time once, perhaps, long ago.

And so, do not tarry. Do not focus upon that which is not in alignment, but focus on those things which will propel your steps forward. Seek insights through meditational ways. Seek that knowingness from within as you engage first, always through the heart center as opposed through mental ponderings. For the mental-ness will not get you there. It will reinforce that which is not. It will reinforce that which is more, perhaps, egoic, but we would say that it will not lead you to where you truly seek to go. For you see, all of the wonderment is there waiting for you to embrace it — waiting for you to recognize it — waiting for you to incorporate it into your being and world as you move in this manner moving forward.

As we proceed, we ask for you to move in that alignment of the oneness of all that is. To move into the alignment of all that might be. To move into the alignment that will help you navigate this life in a way in which you have not navigated before. All life seeks to embrace you in the Loving expanse it does offer. And it is only the awareness, and the wanting, and the looking, and the desiring of that which is to be — that all might be more readily attained.

And so this is what we seek this day: that you will look at life in the wonderment that it is. That you will not be caught and trapped within the dramas of the day. That you will move beyond what appears to be taken from you in the injustice that does seemingly exist.

And recognize that there must be a right and wrong in order to see the good and the bad, in order to see the wanted and the unwanted, so that there is a feeling component that you can align with and know that this is preferred and this is not. For if only light were shown, there would not be the diversity or the differing mannerisms of that which was sought in a way that was not known before.

For you see, if you knew these things, you would not be here. If you knew these things, you would not have taken embodiment. And so recognize that the converse was necessary so that you might have the full expanse of the totality of that which you sought to know. And so that is the purpose of the diversity, and perhaps perceived negatively, that does exist, but when you do so — when you view each, when you engage with the knowledge that this is a part of the plan, then you can look upon it differently. And you do not feel that you have been imposed upon or infringed upon, but now you look upon it as an opportunity for expansion.

And that is what we seek to impart here. That is what we seek for you to know. That is what we seek for you to do and embrace in a more conscious way so that all the dots are connected … so that in this lifetime, you do so in the consciousness and the Loving embrace in which many of these activities exist. For we would say those activities that you believe to be of a negative nature are, as we have said before, gifts. Gifts to be recognized, unwrapped, and seen for what they truly are.

And when you move in this manner, when you move in this awareness, when you move in this way, life appears differently. And now you look at life in the conscious awareness in which you now exist, and it becomes surreal. It no longer feels heavy, weighted, and in the density in which it is. For that is the Earth experience. For without the full feeling component, there is not the potentiality of the possibility for more to be known in this way.

And so move this day in this way, and see how your day does unfold. See how your day does unfold, and how the beauty of the day then can progress, and be all that it might be, had aligned to be, in this wanting as it wafts and floats about. Anchor now and know moving forward that more is to be given.

Moving into Alignment

As we proceed, further anchor in Light and Love moving forward in the wonderment of what might be. We will say there is much which is known, but much more which remains unknown, and that which is on the precipice of entry back into this world of form. For it has been remiss or missing from being recognized in this time and space.

And so as you anchor into these words

and into all that is, know that it is in many regards a remembrance of what was once known and understood intrinsically. And so allow yourself to read and hear these words, and for a bubbling up to occur within your system. For it is in many ways the allowing of what was once known and understood to be recalled, remembered, and once again gleaned as a part of the understanding from which you operate.

There is this component, known as the body vessel. And the body vessel anchors and harbors much. And as we have touched upon and talked about in the *Awaken* book *(Awaken to Manifest Your Best Life)*, there is much that occurs within the day and within the facilitation of the body that occurs without thought or interjection by you, conscious awareness.

As you consider and muse upon this now, might you recognize that it is a rather large undertaking — that you ingest food, digest food, shift, adjust within the day to activities and undertakings that cause your body to need to effortlessly shift from one mode into the next. And we would like for you to consider that now for just a moment as you conceptualize all that your body does undertake and move to embrace within the day. Might you do so now?

∾ *Conceptualization Pause* ∾

As you reflect here once again, might you see that it is a rather large undertaking and that were you to need to incorporate instruction and direction, as far as perhaps your heartbeat and the regulation of your blood flow, that this would be an ongoing process? For you see, each must occur ongoing and effortlessly throughout your day. And so were that to be the objective, and the premise, and the purpose for your activities within the day, you would be engaged as such in a mental mind bog to have this or that activity occur.

And so consider further, as you move about and perhaps you take a tumble or run a race, and now you are out of breath, or have another occurrence within your system that you must stop and regulate, how this would further layer upon that which is.

And then to take it even a step further as you consider the emotional energy that becomes anchored and stored within your body ... that this energy is gathered and accumulated within this form. And it does then shift and change all that was there before. And as this becomes recognized, and as this becomes quantified, you then must address this or that energetically. And you do see that all of this would take time in order for you to process and to adequately maintain.

As you muse and consider this further, we ask for you to recognize that your body, its importance, and the vessel from which you know as your being or your personality, is intertwined with that Spiritual Essence which did then enter in, and commingle one with the other, so that you are able to experience life in the densities in which life does exist here.

It is as if you were putting on a spacesuit to go out and do a spacewalk that you need certain components in which to breathe. You need certain components in which to move and navigate about. You need certain components in which you might exist in the reality in which you find yourself.

There is the one, the vessel — the body form — and there is the other, the Pure Conscious Awareness. And the two were needing to merge and meld together so that there might be the full totality of experience in a more seamless and effortless way. And so you see, there are those writings which have discussed the vessel in a more complete form. And so you might research that if you prefer more than what we will give and provide here.

There is the body vessel. Within the body vessel, there are certain characteristics and properties that are maintained mentally. And the mental aspect, which we have stressed before and others have done so as well, that is not a part of the Conscious Awareness from which you reside … there is that incessant and compelling dialog that does routinely occur.

It is advisable to always respond to the mental understandings and underpinnings in a way of reflection, but not in a way of owner-ship. For these do continue on incessantly. In recent times, there has been more of an understanding that this mental prodding is a part of that which is considered self. And we now want you to consider that this is *not* a part of you. It is separate and aside from you and it is nothing that need be maintained, judged, or engaged with in any way other than the recognition that it does exist.

We further want to recommend that when these mental opinings occur, that you reflect upon them and consider briefly if it is something moving from a more conscious awareness standpoint, or that small voice that also operates within, or if it is more of a demanding egoic measure that you need to place aside, chuckle at, and continue on … for we will also say that the mind is *not* you.

The mind is and does relegate the activities of the body, and that body vessel does need maintenance 24/7. And do you see, because the maintenance occurs from morning until night and then in between while you sleep, that this mental voice also operates within that same time parameter? But it is meant to be something that you use as a tool. But not knowing that it is a tool, the tool has taken over the assembly line.

And so we would say also that as you

consider this and that, that you recognize that it is like the computer taking over at the location where the mainframe is in play. And in that consideration, that the computer is now running that which the operator should be running. And the operator is standing by as the computer does orchestrate what plays and occurs and what programs are run while the operator sits and listens patiently to what the computer might advise.

We would encourage then for that to be shifted. And for you to recognize that this is not the design that was originally set up within the formatting and planning of this enterprise and in this collaboration … for there is, in many ways, a collaboration of what is occurring.

There is the body vessel, and there is the

Spiritual Consciousness. And the two were needed, are needed, in order for the operation to seamlessly and effectively occur within the existence here. And do you recognize that over time the awareness has been lost of the intricacies and the connection between the two?

And so we do want you to know that the awareness might be recognized once again. For you are not the body vessel, you are not the mind. You are not those things which appear to be you because within the densities that exist here, you needed that spacesuit in order to breathe, in order to navigate, in order to exist in the time and space in which you now reside. And so, not knowing these things, not recalling, and existing through multiple incarnations having let go of that which you cannot see, we want you to recognize this once again. For it will help with the under-standing, and the compartmentalizing, and the releasing of the mental egoic voice that is so incessantly playing within the background of your day.

As you consider life, and as you consider different opportunities, and certain things are interjected, or incessantly pronounced within the playings and the activities that the mind does profess, we want you to recog-nize that it is not real, that it is unnecessary, and that you chart your own course. But you must be aware that the mind is not you. So that when it recommends this or that, when it suggests different activities that take you off-course or in a different direction than you might otherwise be, we want you to be the conscious awareness. We want you to be consciously aware of what it is doing. And in that conscious awareness, you can then consider life and the things that are suggested mentally in a different way.

For it is in the understanding, and the perceptions held that you then can make different choices within life because now you no longer see life through the limited mental scope in which you may have seen life before. For how were you to know that the mental promptings that you have been receiving are not your own? And we would say to consider the body vessel as a large computer with various programs and various considerations that must be prompted, refueled, energized, and kept in play.

Yet you, as conscious awareness, are a being that needs to be refueled, but it is through the stilling of the mind. It is through the separation from the mind. It is from the resetting and restoring of that which was understood much more easily before.

So now consider the body vessel and consider the Soul Awareness. And that they do meld and merge together in the oneness in which they now reside within this Earth plane, and within the dynamic of the day and within the doings of the day. And how they do ceaselessly communicate and work together. Yet, there are those components that take the body vessel down a path that would make it harder for it to operate and be in the polarity and the oneness of all that it might be and all that it is.

And so those choices made throughout the day of what to eat, what to drink, what to ingest, what to participate in, what to play in, what to activate or not within the system are those components which either elevate and fortify or diminish and retard. And so throughout the day, it is greatly recommended that you stay consciously aware of all that you are fueling within the choices, and the opportunities, and the components that are enlisted from those things that are selected for you to participate in, ingest and enjoy.

We do not suggest that you live a puritanical life or that you limit all types of foods at all times. But we would say that limiting what you ingest and doing so in a more conscious way is the solution, in many cases, to negative issues that seem to arise when there is no curfew given to the teenager who engages in activities they know are not advised.

As you consider foods and different varieties of those things that you choose to ingest, know that all will fuel your body accordingly. And so, you will want to research those food groupings that will facilitate the best flow for your form. Know that as you incorporate these new considerations, or existing ones into your daily dealings, that it will infuse your body in a way perhaps that it has not been fueled before. For you see when you do things from a conscious awareness standpoint, and you move into the flow of the day, incorporating beneficial components into your choices and into your selections, your body has the benefit of these choices and selections.

You need not be concerned and overly cautious as you move about to experiment with this or that but rather to see how your body responds when you shift and change what goes into its form. Digestion and other considerations will more easily occur when different food groupings are chosen or time is considered as to when, and how often, and how much to eat. You see, these are all components that help to fuel the body in a more appropriate way.

As you move about within this day and you choose those different food groupings that benefit the objective from which you move now amongst the day, might you say it is to maintain a healthy vessel, a healthy body, and one that will propel you forward in the later years of your life?

For if you move as earlier in life, with no consideration for your later years, you may burn the candle at both ends and find that when you move about to focus on a more purpose-driven outcome, that there is not the body capacity to fulfill what you wish to accomplish.

And so this is the rationale and the preference of protecting and supporting the body; it is that you work in coalition and in collaboration with this vessel form. And that you recognize that it is temporary. It is something that is not carried with you from this life to the next. And so it is a temporary container that does house many things for your use throughout this lifetime. But if you do not recognize and see it as a temporary form, then you may not take the proper care and maintain the best oversight of this vessel.

So what might you do as you consider food choices? And as you are about and in the day, how will you enlist better choices? For the mind does prompt you to try this and try that and *mmmm* how good this would taste and how another would be so worthwhile and perhaps make life more fun. And especially when considering drugs and other stimulants of a nature that are not of benefit, how do you enlist oversight so that the choices are those that are preferred and will allow for the maximum usage of this body vessel?

For you see, you find yourself in a collaboration. You find yourself in the mix of wanting to know how this or that might feel — yet not perhaps knowing the full outcome of the choices in the time in which you make the determination. And what about considerations of addiction, of those things ingested? Might you now move to recognize that those too must be a consideration of the choices that you then enlist or not into the daily dealings of what, we will say, is life here?

And so enjoy those things that you see, and you would like to try, but do so in small measure. And when you recognize if they impose an ill effect upon you mentally, which is to say on your body, then you might move away from larger quantities that might take you down a path that would be harder to reverse or not embark upon in a bigger way the next day.

In other words, sometimes cravings magnify and grow and become that which is unsustainable for the body to perform its daily dealings and duties to maintain life here as you know it and enjoy it. And so be the good steward of your body vessel and form so it might anchor you into the objectives, into the accomplishments you set out to understand and know once, perhaps long ago.

And now we shift slightly to another topic

within the same parameter, but we ask for you to consider this in a more whimsical way so your mind might get around something it may not otherwise understand. We ask you to consider now a third dynamic within the mix of these dealings. We ask for you to consider not only the body vessel and the Conscious Awareness that do navigate to intertwine together, but a third component not often discussed or understood. Consider now a third ingredient into the mix of the dynamics of this body, or might we say personality — for the personality does incorporate many things. It does incorporate the vessel, the Conscious Awareness, and that unknown third ingredient that oversees the mix and is the glue that holds it all together.

We would say to move into that alignment

so that you might be receptive to receive. Move into the alignment and the knowingness that so much is unknown, that much has been lost in time, and that we are in the time and space to bridge that awareness of what is yet to be because it already is, do you see? Do you see that there is that which is in existence, but perhaps unknown to the mental knowingness — that we would say is the mental egoic knowingness of what is understood within the day?

Now we shift into that discussion so that you might have a greater awareness of what this body does truly harbor in addition to those known ingredients. We move to discuss the third, the Intrinsic Knowingness, and the Overseer of all. That component is the source and the energy from which you are derived.

And it is Source Energy that collaborates amongst the two to bring them into the fruition you see within the personality that does aspire to achieve in this platform.

Source Energy — God Source — is the glue that brings the two together and keeps this body, what we might say, functioning, and operating, and alive. For without the three components working in unison and in union together, there would not be the functioning of the body with the consciousness as Source Energy is the glue.

Chapter 3

Shifting Sands of Time

Within life and the complexities found within the day-to-day dealings with life in general, you will find that much is not as it is presumed to be. And in fact, much of what the mind presumes is factually incorrect. And so, as you enlist to learn and discover more, you will have, let us say, a degree of backlash from the mind, in that the mind does seek to control and navigate the vessel which it has now commandeered. It does seek to circumvent, to a degree, you attaining that knowledge, for it is in many ways the diminishment then of the mind and mind's control over the vessel.

And do you see at many levels, there is a control issue at play within life in general by those who orchestrate grander objectives for those who are inhabitants here, but then again also mentally by the mind which does navigate the vessel in how it does proceed and what it does perceive.

If you enlist from the wonderment of a child those steps that will enable you to look upon the vessel and the activities that surround the vessel, then you remain consciously aware and in more of a questioning mode. Not in a needy way of asking because you do not know and are fearful, but in a wonderment sort of way. In the general parameters of the loveliness and the potentialities that might otherwise be in existence were you to allow them to be.

For do you see that the mind is a dicey deal? The mind seeks to circumnavigate and circumvent the awareness from regaining enough awareness to seek a recapturing or a reckoning of losing its grasp and grip over the vessel which it now has commandeered and controls.

And so you must want this much more than you do perhaps at this point in time. For if you had wanted it previously, you would perhaps not be in the mind game in which you find yourself. And so we seek now to start with this rather than that. So that as you set about to listen, read, or understand what is being given, you do so with more clarity because you understand the constraints with which these words might be received if you do not recognize that there will be opposition to the understanding of them.

And so you may choose to put this book down. You may choose to not listen any longer. You may choose to place this book back upon the shelf to inquire and learn more another day. And this is where we would say that you must push through a degree of this — push through what is now rising to the surface. Push through the inclination to no longer listen or intently digest these words.

For you see, the mind is a dicey deal, and it does seek … control. And it does seek to take control, maintain control, and be in control of all that moves forward within your life. For that is its program; that is its intent. That is its relentless and unpausing nature.

You as conscious awareness must, at this point, navigate appropriately so that it does recognize that there is another captain that has now joined the ship. And that captain seeks to run things a little bit differently. And so do seek to know that the captain is in control and does so with Loving measure. Does so in reverence of what is in the midst of all who recognize what is in play and underway.

We seek for you to know that with the three components that join together to bring life into this body and allow your Spiritual Consciousness to navigate in this terrain, we let you know that there is a purpose that was devised once long ago. And that purpose would allow that Spiritual Consciousness to enact and know an energy that It did not quite understand in a physical way. It did not quite understand how this or that energy would feel were It to step into a position of knowing. And so, It sought to expand and know more.

There was an agreement that was entered into by the Soul, as there are certain parameters by which the Soul must agree … before entering into this Earth platform. So it is not an accident. It is not as a result of a misunderstanding. There is a clear path and a clear understanding of what was wanted — is wanted and is now in play. And we seek for you to remember components of this. Perhaps not mentally for that has been blocked, but to have a sense or feeling that this is so.

And so, we seek this day for you to engage

in such a way that you enter into a contemplative mode to feel the words that are evoked rather than to mentally try to decipher what is being given. This, to some degree, is resisted. And so, it is truly the incorporating of the words at a more intrinsic level that will get you to where you seek to go.

Recognize there was an agreement. And in this agreement, you would garner certain things similar to donning a spacesuit, as we interjected previously. And by donning this spacesuit, you could breathe within the environment, you could blend in with other inhabitants who operated there and who operate there, and you could accomplish what you seek and sought to understand.

In addition, you are given and have with you an unseen entourage which we have referred to in previous times. And there is no set number within your entourage, but they are not seen, oftentimes not known, and they do enter into the stage of your life when you invite them in.

And that invitation comes in the form of prayer, asking insightful questions, meditative or contemplative questions, questions before you go to sleep at night, or those ponderings that you engage with throughout the day. For now you are in seeking mode, and they await that opportunity because at that time you are receptive to receive.

And so, we have referred to them as the great mimickers. We have referred to them as the ones that do step in to enlist answers when perhaps you've called to another. For it is their opportunity, you see, to delve into assisting what they know you have intrinsically requested. And that is why you hear and have known that God Source, or such a source as Source Energy, or some other title used to represent Omnipotence and that OmniPresent Power that is about you and about this space all of the time.

For you are, they are, and All that is does operate with that Spark of Divinity. And so, it is simply that you have donned a robe of mortal-dom while on this planet. So that you could experience what you did not understand previously, and this is why you are here. This is why you chose to come into physical form. So that you could know the extremes of that which you sought to know, so that you knew more of the depth of which that thing is.

We will say that the thing that is the

creative production of the energy you sought to create is the byproduct of what it is you want to understand. And so don't you see that you can be doing it in any number of ways? It is the energy that you keep in the doing. And so if the thing that you once loved no longer feels as it once did and now feels sticky, dense, weighted, heavy, unwanted, then you must release that and move on to this other thing. This thing that makes your heart sing. This thing that makes you feel that all is possible and makes you look forward to the next day, and gives you that bounce within your step … don't you see?

And so, it is all about the feeling component. And when the feeling component shifts, you must shift-change too. You must shift-change so that you can mirror this rather than that as you move your alignment to be in oneness with something that is preferred.

We would say there is a degree of inwardly knowing this. But sometimes you are in the midst of one activity or another, or living in one spot rather than another, or in existence in a way that turns into something that is not preferred, and you resist the change that is required for you to move back into that Loving embrace, that Loving space, that space that you might enlist that would give you that more preferred feeling energy.

This is the present moment awareness that is so critical or is so important for you to understand and maintain. For if you are mentally engaged and are in a mind activity most of the time, you do not acknowledge that these things do not feel as they might or as they should. And we seek for you to regain a measure of that once again. We seek for you to regain the proximity of Love and Loving embrace that you must maintain, to a degree, so that you can navigate this life more appropriately, and make better choices, and see better options, and enlist better perspectives. So that your perspectives are those which make you feel better to be in the space in which you reside.

And that is what we seek to impart here. For the agreement is simply with this unseen entourage that they navigate you in a more appropriate way that keeps you, in many regards, directed to the right choices that will move you and keep you in alignment with the Agreement that was established so long ago.

The Agreement keeps you on the path toward your original purpose. The difficulty yet is that in this day, most know about the life purpose but very few recall or engage with their original purpose. And we have explained it in a number of ways, but let us say in the newness of this space that there are life purposes that are given within each embodiment, and they have a component or a degree of understanding that are a component of the original purpose. But until the original purpose is enacted, there is the returning to complete what was begun once, perhaps long ago.

And so there is no timetable for completion, for you see you did come from a space of no time. And time here is another illusionary component, for there is simply energy and a boundless opportunity to engage — to learn what is wanted.

When Soul Essence entered into form,

there was not the concern that this or that would take a long time to gather or ascertain. And in fact, many thought that the original embodiment would facilitate all they sought to know. The difficulty here was that the densities that they entered into were greater than they perhaps understood previously. And they did not anticipate how things would feel. And they did not anticipate what the mind would impose within the space of not knowing. For it was not an elevated instruction that was given. It was more of a fight or flight or rudimentary sort of instruction that was imposed upon this delicate life force.

And so that, coupled with ego, entered in to give something other than the pure Love and direction that might otherwise have been proffered. And so many times the life force in that original incarnation did pass either abruptly or from a lackluster response to the various energetic components that were in play. And by this we mean, oftentimes, there was so much coming at the one that they did not move as they might have believed while spiritually placed, for the densities felt here are felt in a different way and are much more significant than perhaps previously believed.

Know this day, that as you listen, as you read, as you understand this from the platform from which you now reside, that you have been incarnating perhaps for quite a time. And so we seek that you marinate with this, and you then be the marinade within it so that you understand what is being given.

Might you pause now in meditative contemplation, focusing first on your heart space and recognizing that questions posed might begin from that space as opposed to mentally? For the mental space will leave you adrift and give you confirmations that are not preferred, for they will move you more in a mental premise than in a heart space premise. And will give you answers that will require additional insights and direction later, for they do not take you on the direct route you seek.

Seek now to know from that Loving embrace, from that Loving space that you have carried within and is still accessible even in this day. For it is always with you, it is always about you, and it is always ready to place you in the best footing for what might now be as you move beyond this space and into that Loving embrace.

As you enlist a meditational pause, might you listen to uplifting music and then ask to know more? Have a journal or laptop near you. And so as you ask the question — *Might I know more?* – allow the answer that appears to come into your awareness, and then write it down. Write down anything else that comes in during this time. We would say that although the music may not be engaged here, you might play musical engagements on your own as you focus upon the question:

Why am I here, and what now might I know to engage this process in a manner that will allow me to know more … allow me to move in unrestricted ways to engage what I once sought to understand more deeply?

Pose questions, elicit answers, and know the answers are coming forth because you have willed them out of their dormant space, their private space, their proximity into the nowness of this time.

❦ Meditational Pause ❦

We seek for you to know that there is more than what you may physically or mentally perceive. And so we move forward to provide additional components that are necessary for you to have the full encapsulation, the full personification, the full understanding of what this body, this life, this experience, and how it has been assembled, how it has been extrapolated, how it has occurred. We seek for this to be known by you once again.

And so, do you see that all life is a mystery in many ways? For there are many presumptions and assumptions as to how you got here and why you are here. And also how your body is and how it came to be.

We will say it is not of that lowly design that is promoted oftentimes, but it is a higher design and a design that was brought about so that you might experience life in the full totality that it might be — in the lightness of being of which it is. But sometimes, there are choices made that facilitate changes within the body — that spark and ignite different potentialities to be in cue and in existence. And so, these do alter what was perhaps planned upon or established formerly.

Know that as you navigate and move about here, and as you circumnavigate sometimes the globe of this world, there are things that you experience and see, and there are other components that exist within the mix of your day and in the background of activities and of surroundings that are not apparent or as perceived.

There are many levels to this life which you live. You perhaps travel and go somewhere where there is a familiarity and a comfort level in reaching that location. Yet this location was formerly unknown. And we have discussed this in the *Awaken* book, but we would say that there are deeper components to those pathways you travel and experiences that perhaps were sought formerly or in another period in time, and there is an energy that perhaps still emanates there that does ebb and flow within the mix of the day and within all that does exist, having reconnected to that energy once again.

Know that as you ponder these things, that life will continue to be that mystery. That wonderful enterprise that is not fully known or conceptualized by the mind and the limitations imposed by the mind, for it cannot conceptualize many things beyond its immediate parameter of understanding.

As you move about in this life, and you seek to incorporate new understandings, the mind sometimes rejects or does not hear what is brought forward. And so we would say to allow sometimes the words and the insights to permeate and to saturate and then to allow the bubbling up of the intrinsic understanding that does result. It is the deeper, more recognized, more wanted feeling component that does then emanate from there.

Life is and does equate the result of anticipation sought. The result of anticipation sought and what is to then be gleaned. For each is that which it is and awaits entry into your understanding and into this world of form.

So as you think about the body mechanics and the body vessel per se, and you recognize that it has many duties that you may not be fully aware of, having perhaps covered them in school or not, or having recognized that it is a complex organism that does require oversight and guidance, good fueling, good tooling, good mechanisms that keep it operational and functional throughout the duration of the mechanism or organism that is now in consideration and play.

We will say that when you leave this life,

and there is no longer the need for the vessel, the vessel then does decay, for it is no more — for the activation component was the Soul Essence. The Soul Essence commingled with the Source Energy. It did provide life and the merging and melding together of the three-in-one.

As you consider this further, recognize that a Soul is needed to encapsulate that which did not need encapsulation before … for Spirit Essence is unbounded and is unlike as perhaps perceived, but when it moves into the body form, it does need that Soul encapsulation. And so, there is a minimization in the process from the expansive energy, into Soul, into body.

As you muse upon this now, consider the vastness of being which your being has been and will soon again be. For life does have an ebb and flow, and there is much, much more to life in general than simply this life. For you did come from a vastness of understanding, and in that totality of being, you did want to seek more. You did want to understand and know what something felt like. You wanted to know what something felt like and how it would be to experience this or that emotional energy … this or that emotional energy, this or that experience, this or that activity, this or that creation.

And so, you did then become a co-creator in form — a co-creator here on this planet, in this planetary system, in this world. And you are more, as we will always say, than you may believe to be … for there has been indoctrination that you are not of a high level but of a more lowly way and understanding. And we would say that this is not so. There may be actions taken that are not of the highest order, but this platform of experience was meant to be understood. It was meant to be understood and recognized, conceptualized, and then embraced or not by the feeling component, which you gauge throughout your meanderings on this planetary system and world.

Do recognize that there is that reckoning and that understanding, but it has been misinterpreted and reformulated, and perhaps reimagined, for there is not that full understanding but the presupposing that you are less than, that you cannot be the full measure of, and that you must relinquish your reign of control for your own body vessel to another or something that is supposed by religious doctrines that limit the expression of who you are and what you are to be.

And so we would say that, although there is no right or wrong within this planetary system in many regards, you must also be the discerner of what is what and who is who. And as you consider this, recognize that you are expansive, unbounded Spiritual Essence that has sought to take a form and to wonder no more. To now know in more certainty, or more precise mannerisms and ways, how it would be and how it would feel, to do thus and such, create thus and such, or exist simply here.

As you move about this day, look upon life as an experience. Look upon life, removing the limitations felt of what you might be able to do or not, what you might be able to experience or not, in what way and how you might exist or not, in this platform of wonderment, opportunity, and being.

Chapter 4

Purposeful Understandings and Their Undertakings

Might we begin this next chapter in a two-fold way? One, let us begin this next chapter, but also might you begin your next chapter. As you recognize that the body, the Soul, and Source Energy have come together to join this body form to facilitate what you sought to understand once before, might you recognize that there is much more within the mix of this understanding, and what will be given as we proceed?

Know that Universal Love is the key, in many regards, to all you might want to facilitate. Universal Love, as we have said, is a healing component that might be engaged in this day in a more purposeful way so that energy might be shifted in a way that you might express all you intend or intended to at one point in time.

And so how to determine the purpose you seek to find? How to determine that thing which perhaps you have only recently discovered existed? For you say, *the life purpose has been a question for quite a time, but now I have not only the life purpose but also the original purpose in which to ponder and query a question.*

And so we would say that the original purpose is the greater component and is the reason that so many have not been able to leave the Earth platform, for it is a component that must be completed for you set up the components by which the completion might occur. And so if you have not checked off all the components that would allow for that completion to exist, then you have, by the agreement that was made once, returned to consider yet again reaching that alignment and fulfilling what you set out to understand and explore once before.

We would say that once before may have been a multiple type of query or may have occurred in multiple steps in multiple times. But there is no exact formula and no exact amount of time that you need to spend on this platform except to be able to get into the flow of the awareness of what you seek to understand and sought to understand, so then its completion might be recognized.

And it is in the awareness mode of recognition that you might recognize these things would come into form and into being. For to do them and not know that you are doing them, in a manner of speaking, is by happenchance. And it is in the awareness of what you are doing, why you are doing it, and the feeling that is associated with the completion and the actual enterprise of the occurrence that is most meaningful. And so we seek now for you to recognize that this is something that has been long sought. It is because of the maya that does exist around you and the choices that do exist that seem most significant that you perhaps have not accomplished this previously.

Now we seek to share a bit more. Might you consider that in earlier times, there was an agreement? And the agreement was simply that you would do this and accomplish that. And you would recognize this by the feeling evoked in the doing of the activity.

We have spoken about the body vessel, the Spiritual Essence requiring a Soul in which to connect to this body vessel, and Source Energy that, let us say, is the glue that does then keep all components securely together. And so the Agreement is something that we would like to pause and recognize now, as it is quite significant (as) to why you are here, why you have continued to re-embody, and why this life has taken the twists and turns, perhaps, that it has taken as you navigate the many varied life experiences that do exist and have existed in previous times.

The Agreement was formulated so that there was a complete understanding of what would occur and what one might expect when entering into the physicality of this domain. And so there are certain things within the Agreement — the recognition, the understanding, the connection of the dots so to speak — so that as you move and grow and continue to navigate this life that there were certain understandings that would be accomplished.

The Spiritual Essence in the wonderment of what is, felt this was a rather easy occurrence and that it would be easily accomplished in short order. But as we have mentioned, there was not the full understanding of what this Earth experience would feel like and how the full depth of the density here would be felt, we would say, to the core.

And we have previously mentioned in other writings, and in this written way, and orally expressed that there was not the depth of understanding for the complexities of the experience and how it would be so fully felt in a most deep way. And as might be understood, it did take the Soul, in many cases, out of embodiment, for there was not the understanding that it would be in quite the way in which it was experienced and felt.

The Soul many times chose to leave the body and leave the experience. And in doing so, there was no longer the recall of that life experience. There was no longer the recall of the specific occurrences but rather the overall understanding that was gleaned in a most expedient way after the life experience had ended.

There was an overview, let us say, given, and an understanding. And as this has occurred repetitively from one incarnation to the next, and then the next, and then the other, there was a diminishment of the recall of that original objective. And although there is an understanding of the life experience and the life purpose, there is not the ready recall of the original one.

And the original one is most necessary because it is the *Original Agreement* that was made to be understood that would relinquish the rounds of reincarnation. That would relinquish and, in a manner of speaking, stop the rotation of incarnations, for the accomplishment at that point will have been completed. We would say it is the full 360-degree return of that which was initiated once upon a time, once long ago.

Once that has come to complete fruition, and the full 360-degree circle is then complete, then the Soul is no longer tethered in this way, do you see — to experience that which It sought to understand and to be understood. And so, understanding that there is an agreement, understanding that you were a participant of the Agreement, is most relevant and noteworthy.

Additionally, you were given those who would travel with you for a safe journey and would be those that you could call upon when you needed answers to questions. And the means of connection was simply that you would still the mind and connect. And initially, that was more easily attained. Yet over time, again, these beings were not seen. And so there, at this point in time, is not the recall that they do exist, although you have heard of Guardian Angels and the like. They do then travel with you to assist in answering questions. To assist to help you in many unseen ways. But you must be open to their assistance, or else how do you know you are getting that assistance or actually employing that which is beyond your mental knowingness.

We again will say that there is not a set or specific number, but we would add to say that there are usually four or five beings that are with you at all times. And of course, this number can increase because sometimes the

Soul did bring Others from their dimension who did volunteer to stand behind and assist in an unseen way.

But we will say that each do have a vested interest in facilitating objectives for the Soul when the Soul is receptive to recognize that they are doing so and is looking consciously for answers that have been given that await discovery and recognition in the time and space in which they are allowed entrance. And that entrance is allowed through recognition, and conscious awareness, and employing, as we have said in other times, that ability to look and sleuth out the answers. And so will you recognize there is an agreement in place that Universe does maintain and does so Lovingly for the life experience you have asked and requested to enjoy and employ?

And so, this is the Earth platform and the means by which you understand this life occurrence. And we will say that when you cannot see these things and there is not the recall, and there is not the awareness, and there is not the early training from childhood, it is hard to know to pause the mind to elicit these things into your awareness simply because you do not know that they exist … so how do you know you must elicit them to bring them forward?

It is a quandary, let us say, and something that is not expected, or anticipated, or brought forward in a manner that would cause you to chuckle and recognize that there are many things that are yet unknown to the mind. And so this is why we say you must step, and sidestep, and bypass the mind so that you do not limit yourself to mental ponderings or mental understandings.

We will say that because you do not recall many aspects in one time or the other that there is the inability to incorporate that which might make this Earth experience a bit easier. For if you did recall these things and knew that it was a priority, you would immediately shift your activities to do this rather than that.

But part of the journey is the discovery. Part of the journey is the mystery. Part of the journey is the unanticipated occurrences that do exist when you are here. For if you knew all these things initially, would you live your life the same way and have the same experiences that you can now claim to recall at this point in time? In other words, would you dare to dream to the extent if you knew that this was it? If you knew this was it, and you needed to enact, or do, or feel this certain thing, would you then just circumvent the other portion of the experience to get to that?

In many ways, that was the rationale of keeping this a bit cloaked, might we say. But now you have been here for a time, and more time, and there is no longer the recall. There is no longer the recall that you came to experience this or that, but really it is more that you have now become trapped within the maya that does exist within this experience and other experiences that have occurred before.

Will you recognize that although you may believe that this cause or that cause is the best thing and is something that you must get behind because perhaps you have an abundant life, and perhaps you feel that you must now give back, which we say is a good thing to do. But might you also realize that it is time to get about why you came here? For now, you have had many experiences and many opportunities, and many timelines and lifetimes of discovery. And now it is the time to move all of this forward to get about why you came here in the first place.

It is in the understanding of the three-in-one component within your body vessel, your Soul Essence, and Source — it is important to understand that they are unique and distinctly separate, one from the other. And although Soul is, in essence, Spiritual Essence and a part of Source Energy, it has taken on a form of the Soul, which makes it uniquely distinct from the other.

It is when these three come together in

their formation and in the causation that does allow the experience to exist in the way, and in the manner in which it does, that you then are able to be a part of this earthbound adventure. That you are able to be a part of it in a way that blends you in to others who also are experiencing that which they perhaps are unaware, having come from a different location than the one they might suppose.

And so seek now this day to have the full understanding of what is in your future. And it is in the slowing and stilling of the mind that you can get about to find that purpose. It is in the separation of recognizing that you are not the mind — that you are not the body — that you are something more intangible than tangible — something spiritual in nature that is not equated to the physicality in which you find yourself now.

Recognize this and realize that it is for a purpose that you are here. It is for this unique purpose that you have devised, that you have come into form, and that you are experiencing the life that you have thus far experienced in this lifetime, and others, so that you might have a fuller understanding of all the different aspects that you sought to know once long ago.

We wish for you to know that there are aspects which will help you move in a manner so that you will uncover your original purpose much more quickly. And yes, we have talked about looking at childhood preferences, and those things which you sought to do before life's limitations were placed upon you. But we also seek for you to divest yourself of the mental meanderings of your mind … for the mind does impose many of the limitations that you find in this day. And we hope first that by recognizing that the mind is a part of the body vessel, that you will understand the distinction of why the mind is not you … for you are pure consciousness. You are consciousness and not of the physicality that the vessel and all of its components are derived.

When you recognize that you have the ability to do much more than you may currently believe … that is the first step. For you see the recognition that you need not have the limitations that the mind has, up to this point, imposed by slowing and stopping, or stilling it for a time, then you can get about to locate that which is much more difficult without having done so. And it is much more difficult when you do not know the proper steps to take or the way in which this can be attained or achieved. And yes, you can still the mind and engage the little voice to give you the insights sought, but might there be another methodology that you might enlist and engage this day?

Might a new methodology come into play that you might engage so that you might more readily locate that which is seemingly remote, distant, or unattainable? What might that be? What might that methodology be that you could employ to activate and engage that which has been missing for a time and more time?

We expressly wish to impart an understanding which may be familiar or maybe new to you. And so, as you seek to align in this way, know there is always more that you might delve into and understand. But it is in the receptivity to receive that which is offered that often blocks the moving forward or advancement. For the mind can only calibrate or understand in a limited way.

When you seek to understand something more, we ask that you put the mind aside and perhaps adjacent to you and see it as separate from you. And that you implement any step that will allow it to move as if on a conveyor belt beyond and away from you, yet never totally detached, but let us say separate from you for a time.

And it is so there might be a greater understanding conceptualized and absorbed by this aspect of you — the personality which is in existence now. And so, will you take some deep breaths, holding to a count of three and then releasing to a count of three, so you do this for a time? And then re-engage here when you are ready to proceed with this understanding.

∽ *Meditational Pause* ∽

Now that you have paused and allowed a space to be in existence … a space to be in existence from where you were before the space did occur. Might you recognize that there are understandings that you can employ to speed up the process to access that which you seek in all regards? And as you seek, so you will find.

And so, because it has been asked repetitively for this to be brought forward, it is now being brought forward into this time and space so that more might be anchored here in a way of discovery and personal truth — that these truths might perhaps set you free from the rounds of incarnation and those things that have been adopted but need not be. Need not be adopted, or implemented, or continually engaged in the rapidity of what they suggest. And let us say perhaps, what they are presumed to evoke and provoke.

For often, there is that understanding that is not real. That you must do this or that, or engage in a certain way when there is always free will, and that free will opportunity to shift-change what is placed before you. But when you do not know, or when you presume that you know all in that space, and you do not ask for more, then there is not the opportunity for more to be engaged.

Now that you have shifted, and aligned as you might, and allowed that mental pause to be engaged, and you have moved the mental knowingness aside, and out of direct correlation with what might be, we will share some unique insights that you might engage and employ and place within the day so that you align in a more specific way, and in a way that will produce all you seek, do you see?

As you have shifted the mind out of its cradle, and its position of power that arches over the body form and is that which seeks to know all, but cannot, for it is limited by the parameters by which it operates, might you move now to embrace Source Energy? That you go directly to Universe and that which is a part of the three-in-one to specifically ask in a firm but definitive way for more to be employed.

We would say as you sit in that posture, you enlist action, for this has been told before. We wish to add a caveat to it to make it even more impactful and meaningful as you navigate your day. For you see, as you engage with Source, and as you mirror the demanding yet not demanding voice and posture of enlisting that which you know to be so, enlisting that which you know is your right to know, enlisting the measure that is for your purposeful adventure to be completed and moved into its completion mode, might you sit with this query as you engage to enlist a mantra that will move this into proximity so that the mind does cease to exist, for a time, and you can then more readily connect to that which is your heart's desire? That which is your heart's means of connection. That which is more readily proffered into this three-dimensional platform. For now, you are anchoring it with a key of sorts that does unlock the energetic combination to relinquish that which is tightly held for your being and world.

This combination (when) given in sequential rhythm and Love, multiple times, and we would suggest three, it then turns — resets, turns — resets, turns and then opens the portal for you to know intrinsically, as you focus there, what it is you sought once long ago.

For you see, life is as you wish it to be. Life is that which it is, but it is so much more. It is in the wanting. It is in the energetic attachment to the desire of wanting to know and making it a pivotal point that you want this more than you want that because it is the energy of your alignment. It is the energy of your intention. It is the energy of the attention that you place upon this thing that will bring this thing into complete and full manifestation mode so that you intrinsically know ... *this is it*. And then you are able to connect the dots. You are able to anchor that which was and is within your blueprint of design ... for there is nothing beyond your reach. There is nothing beyond your power. There is nothing that you need not know now, for you have willed it, you have willed it into being. You have a willed it to come back and resurface. You have willed it to enter into this arena of life in the here and now — today.

And so, you need not wander the desert, so to speak. You need not wander for any amount of time in the darkness and the depths of wonderment. For now is the time for you to connect, might we say, almost immediately with what you seek to proffer and know. And so, as we impart this understanding, and this mantra, will you then engage it in the wonderment and Love in which it is given? And as you add the component of trust, belief, and feeling into the mix, know that all now is possible. All now is possible as you implement the means in which you do so.

The feeling component, which is most essential, is that you know it to be so, and you accept this gift given. For it is the gift given that you then interpret what is about you, for do you see it is your gift. It is your understanding. It is your knowingness that will propel this to be brought into form. And although there may be a degree of ability to share, and direct, and guide from our vantage of limitless perspective, do you see it is your journey? It is your opportunity. It is your gift that you are to evoke and bring (this) into the physical platform in this world of form.

For to rely on another, and to rely even on Pure Consciousness and that Infinite Awareness that is unlimited and unbounded by knowledge and knowing from the vantage upon which there are insights given, that part of the journey is the discovery of the journey and the recognition that the journey is, how might we say, at the precipice of completion. And the joy of the wonderment of the understanding of what is given, and what is intrinsically received, is a part of that journey in the understanding of it.

And so, move this day. Move this day to know, and to recognize, to feel, and to embrace that which is yours to claim — that which is your energy to evoke. That which is your energy to move forward to Source Energy to say, this is mine, and I will it to know it to be; and to know and be, and have it be that which is known to be and move it now into form. Move it now into the knowingness of this form. Move it into the space where there is no longer the question but the innate, inner knowledge that *this is so*. And this resonates with the one, for it is the one that must resonate back with it. For it is an energetic commingling, do you see, of that which is and is soon to be?

And so we step back now so there is that opportunity to delve into this understanding as you move to embrace an insightful, contemplative, meditative moment to enact and ask for this which is soon to be known — which is now soon to be known — which is now … soon to be known.

Instruction –

*Might you now recite this verse multiple times?
Recite it as given in the manner that will elicit
Universe to hear you. Know it is the recitation; it is
the energy that is invoked. It is the means and methodology for this Energetic Key to become engaged.*

*And so, seek what avenue you might to employ
that which will further anchor the ability for
you to locate that which you seek to find in a
manner and in the Love in which it is given.*

Energetic Key

Let Light and Love remove what's amiss.
Engage that which is now time to enlist.
Move into action so that all might be,
    engaged, aligned, enacted, and freed.

I seek to implore, coax, and kindly demand
    to restore that which is known in-kind and in-hand.
For all which is needed in this space of time,
    does embrace that mystery, both sacred and divine.

For in this day, I do seek and implore
    what is inherent to my being to know evermore.
This holds a measure of what I'm soon to see —
    that which is most integral, essential, vital, and key.

My purpose awaits majestic unto me
    as I undertake to enlist what is soon to be.
For upon recognition when feeling my way,
    I know each thing evoked will move forward
    without delay.

It is this connection that is essential to ascertain,
    while recognizing what is soon easily attained.
I call once again to draw all in-kind,
    to bubble up and resurface —
    that which is intrinsically mine.

I seek ...

- to engage this energetic alignment once more;

- to recognize what I might already be in the *doings* of, as I further explore;

- to release what awaits its cue to resurrect;

- to understand and enlist what has been lost in effect;

- to know that which I now call into full view, as I move to align with all I once knew.

Instruction —

Recite, repeat, then add to complete, singularly, or as you feel so inclined.

Let more now be,
as I align to see
that which has awaited connection and discovery.

Let it be so,
for I am ready, awakened, and wanting to know
what it is time for me to enact, do, and be.

All is Underway

As we move into this next chapter, might you contemplate on what has come before? And might you recognize that all is in the fluidity and flow and in a degree of the acceptance of your mind? For the mind does postulate and formulate and does seek to understand all … for it perceives that it already knows all. And so as you move in this way, and recognize there is more yet to be discovered and so many things are yet to be uncovered, might you move now into this unknowingness with the mental posturing of knowing that more is yet to come?

And so, in this way, we move and progress so that you might conceptualize a bit more. And as we open now and expand the awareness from which you currently reside, might you envision that which we will describe.

Can you see Pure Consciousness, Infinite Awareness, and that which emanates from there, wanting and postulating how this or that might feel … to be? And what does it mean to feel as one does feel in the densities which exist here? We say this is a unique and most opportune opportunity for you to experience and be in the densities of this Earth platform so that you understand how each thing you might contrive and conspire to create does feel in the creation of it. It is a unique opportunity, and one that is most special and prized in many ways — for not all can have that unique aware-ness in a most personal way.

And so, it was this that caused you to move into this platform of awareness and understand-ing. For you see, you did want to understand it in a more unique and personal way because there were those and perhaps are those compo-nents which were still unknown and wanted in a space of knowingness. And so you did enter into the Agreement from which you now reside. So you could posture and formulate pathways of purpose to enable you to see what has been gifted in this Earth journey.

And your journey has been camouflaged, might we say, so that you have the full totality of experience here. So that it is not as if you were merely visiting an amusement park where you know that the rides and the attractions are not authentic, in that you know that you are in the mix (or midst) of some activity that will return you ultimately back to where you reside. For here in this space, you feel as if this is all there is. And so, you are in a total submersion of authentic reality.

But might we say that this reality is not real? It is the unreality from which you reside. And in that lack of true form, you experience that which is not permanent and will soon be placed aside, as where you came from has no time. And so this digression, this moment in history might we say, is but a flash of light. For it does not exist as you believe it to be … as you are here in this space.

Recognize what seems like an eternity is not that. For you came from endless and boundless, expansive enlistments of understanding. For it is here in this space where you must learn and glean that which is intrinsically important to you. And so Universe, Source Energy does say:

Well, if this one does want to know, then they will delve into the understanding and discovery of what is a more firmly footed foundational function and experience or enterprise. They will seek to know more.

And so it is from that space of wanting and sending out the intentional message to discover that which is currently a bit camouflaged and a bit inaccessible in that you must seek to want to know, rather than just merely exist in what appears in your pathway. And so might you know that all in this space is a gift of discovery. For many want to be given their answers, want to be fed and piecemealed their next step. But we tell you that the loveliness, and the bountifulness, and the expression of who you are is for you to discover. It is for you to recognize. It is for you to know when you have moved past the many opportunities and distractions that appear before you.

And when you move in that way, when you move in the way of enlisting what is most preferred and most important to you, then the keys to that understanding will be given. For you must set your vessel and your ship aright. For if you are cocked or moving in a manner that is not in alignment, that does take you off-course and on a detour, might we say, then how can you expect to suppose to land where you might propose to do so this day.

Now we move to progress another understanding that you might conceptualize or not, based on your preference to accept what is given in a Loving and reverent way. Do you see the acceptance and all that has come before is simply a choice? It is your free will choice to elicit a new understanding or to move past it and past these pages and words so that you resonate perhaps with this and not that.

Consider now that this body vessel and this Awareness have been melded and molded and are traversing this Earth, wondering, and plotting, and planning as to how to access that purpose. We will tell you that the verse given, when given in the right manner, and given from a place of conviction from the heart center, is the greatest gift we can give you now. For then, you do move into the wonderment and of the allowing of what is to be resuscitated, might we say, as it re-emerges into this space and platform. For it is your insistence and the energy you evoke to bring your wonderment and understanding that you set up into being once again now.

And so, consider this. Consider this, as you in many ways see and envision this energy bubbling up from within. And then focus upon it. Focus upon it in a contemplative moment with precision, and dedication, and expectation. For if you do not believe it will come, for if you do not believe you have the ability to re-energize and move forward into the light of day those things you once wanted in a strong way, let us say, then how can it ever be reclaimed and regained by you? How can this thing ever return back to you when you do not expect it to be so?

It is in the expectation, the visualization, the meditative moments that you postulate and formulate on this one issue — this one request — this one thing, that it will bubble up and be accessible once again. For in many ways, you have chosen many paths within your lifetime that dance around the occurrence. That dance around what it is that you sought. But rather than one component, one spoke on the wheel, we would say, seek the entire wheel to roll toward you. To be expansive and energetically accessible as you tune your focus into that which is yours to claim. It is yours to know, for it is the experience that you sought to understand

and feel within this earthly domain.

We seek for you to connect there. We seek for you to recognize that this is the gift given within these words and expressions that are now uniquely devised as a key so that you might unlock that which has been with you all along but perhaps not as accessible as you might prefer. For you did not know how to gain access. You did not know how to gain entry. You did not know how to bring forward that which is about you, with you, and within reach — always — all along. And so might you contemplate on this measure for a moment or two before we continue.

Meditational Pause

Now, after your pause, will you be receptive to receive? Be receptive to receive what we offer and give in Loving measure. We seek for you to have a degree of understanding and Love, and knowing that Universal Love is the bridge. It is the bridge to bring you home in many regards. And so when there is that blockage, when there is that inability to connect to receive what you perceive to be that which is rightfully yours to know — it is rightfully yours to experience and to move into that space of expression now that you have discovered its connection, might you know that Universal Love not only is the glue with which Source Energy facilitates the anchoring of your form with your Soul Essence, now known as Soul, but it is also that energy that is the facilitator in many regards of all you seek to know? It is the means and the methodology as well as the integral energy key that will allow your verse to more synchronistically align with you.

Might you return to the verses, or verse, that you received earlier and now recite these verses with the component of Universal Love as its anchoring aspect. Envision it as you recite it, drawing in Universal Love to amplify, might we say, the energetic connection or key that you have been given. And now you align with it even further through the Love component ... through Universal Love.

For it is not merely love as you know. It is not merely the love that is thought of as you know. It is not merely the emotional ingredient of love as you now well know. It is so much more than that ... do you see? And so, now add this ingredient into the mix of that Loving combination we have given you so you might express it in the manner-ism and the way that Universe seeks for you to request what is yours to receive. For don't you see that if you ask meekly, Universe will certainly listen, but you may receive it in a rather meek way. And will you see it in its return to you? But if you do express it boldly, then Universe will pronounce it back to you in such a manner. And you are more likely to see what you need to see, must see, for this manifestation to be known by you in this time.

And so, make an assertive stance. Make an assertive stance in the energy that is most becoming of what it is you want to know. And so in that energy elicit your preference. Elicit the verse. And now do so with Universal Love as your tailwind of support as you enlist it once again now.

Instruction —

*Might you recite this verse multiple times in a way that
will elicit Universe to hear you. Do so in the understanding
you now hold, integrating Universal Love into this key.*

Energetic Key
…Given in Love

Let Light and Love remove what's amiss.
Engage that which is now time to enlist.
Move into action so that all might be,
  engaged, aligned, enacted, and freed.

I seek to implore, coax, and kindly demand
  to restore that which is known in-kind and in-hand.
For all which is needed in this space of time,
  does embrace that mystery, both sacred and divine.

For in this day, I do seek and implore
  what is inherent to my being to know evermore.
This holds a measure of what I'm soon to see —
  that which is most integral, essential, vital, and key.

My purpose awaits majestic unto me
  as I undertake to enlist what is soon to be.
For upon recognition when feeling my way,
  I know each thing evoked will move forward
  without delay.

It is this connection that is essential to ascertain,
  while recognizing what is soon easily attained.
I call once again to draw all in-kind,
  to bubble up and resurface —
  that which is intrinsically mine.

I seek ...

- to engage this energetic alignment once more;

- to recognize what I might already be in the *doings* of, as I further explore;

- to release what awaits its cue to resurrect;

- to understand and enlist what has been lost in effect;

- to know that which I now call into full view, as I move to align with all I once knew.

Instruction —

Now might you …

Recite, repeat, then add to complete
singularly or as you feel so inclined.
Move into cue this day without misstep or delay
in the discovery that awaits you each day.
This is our gift of Love to you.
This love which is now indeed imbued,
as we add a degree of wonderment into the mix.

In Light & Love we do enlist
to engage what has been most remiss
as its reentry does occur in this time.
You see now all is is as it might be
completing the full 360 –
as you recite, repeat, release.

Energetic Key

Let more now be,
    as I align to see
    that which has awaited connection and discovery.

Let it be so,
    for I am ready, awakened, and wanting to know
    what it is time for me to enact, do, and be.

I sit now in contemplation,
    in wonderment, and expectation
    of what this purposeful understanding will reveal.

Each is as it should be,
    and thus I complete the full three-sixty (360),
    as Universal Love has entered in — as the key.

Chapter 6

Completion of Your Journey Here

As we move to encircle that which has come before, know that all is as it needs to be, and as you determine what is to be, might you move with steps accordingly? So that you may bring forward all that you desire, know that your purpose purposefully awaits. It awaits your wanting. It awaits your engagement. It awaits your activation into the knowingness of what this thing, this energy is, and might evoke for you when you are consciously aware of evoking that energy. For you see, you have most probably evoked it before.

Do you see that it is in the conscious awareness of the moment, of the activity, of the engagement, of the need, and want, and desire to have known this energy that you then are moving this energy out into the world of form in a conscious sort of way? You are moving and engaging to know that which is and was unknown before at this level of knowingness. For you see, in many ways, this is the conscious awakening of the being, of the one who is nestled amongst the vessel and propagated, or propelled, or propped up by Source Energy in the alignment of the three-in-one.

Will you look upon life now in the wonderment that it is — in the wonderment that you can engage this or that activity, this or that outcome, this or that undertaking, objective, or mission? But it is when you do so consciously that the engagement becomes evolutionary. It becomes more than what it was thought to be before because now you do so not from the mere enjoyment of it but from the feeling aspect, from the true engagement of what it seeks to elicit to you in this way.

For it is your mission in many ways. It is your mission to accomplish this or that, to do so in a knowing manner, to do so with the knowingness of all that you have set out to accomplish. For you can do many things, but it is in the awareness of the doing that is so critical at this step.

For all you elicit, for all you want, for all that is to be must be done in a manner of knowing that you are doing so. It cannot be happenchance. It cannot be from the mere enjoyment of it, although we do say that life is meant to be enjoyed. But in many regards, it is the connecting of the dots ... don't you see? It is connecting all the dots so that you might complete your mission and return home.

For Earth is a way station. A place where you have landed for a time, but it is not your long-term home. And if you believe in other activities, or other stories, or other past or future occurrences, you might recognize that even in Biblical understandings, you were not meant to be here always.

You were meant to be in a heavenly sort of way when you depart this life. And who is not to say that where you came from is not that heavenly way — is not that portal of potential, and possibility, and promise? For in many ways, you are not the imperfect being that you seem to experience here on this Earth platform because here the imperfections are needed to move you and shift you from this to that.

And that is why it is understood that there is no right or wrong here, for each is propelling you in a direction that is one of preference or not. It is in the proffering of the perspective and in the ability to recognize when a perspective might be shifted and may no longer be neces-sary — that you no longer need to look through it from a limited lens of it being this way or that. For we will say in many regards, the perspec-tive is a part of the journey. The perspective allows you to see things from a limited vantage that are perhaps totally unfounded. But it was needed so that you might move through one and into the next. And so see life, and the perspectives kept, in this regard.

As you look upon another, know that their perspective is necessary for it is their belief. And this is why you might release beliefs. Because when you hold to a belief, and it is steadfast, you need the perspective to reinforce the belief. But when you release the belief, the perspective will yield, and shift, and move to be more in alignment with what might propel you in the next best step.

For do you see that all work in tandem — one with the other — to progress you in a way that will move you to all that your heart is desirous of. And so, if you shift this, then you will shift that. And when you release this, you will release that. And it is like a gridlock of locks. That as you go through the portal, you change the combination a bit. And in changing the combination, the gridlock is no longer in a gridlock sort of way. And now it moves to open. And you go through the next portal, and you work through that. And it opens. And you go through the next, and it opens. And all of a sudden, you see that you are before all that you seek to know. For you have allowed and shifted, and moved, and released what need not be held onto anymore at this point in time.

But all were necessary, do you see? All were necessary to move you into that space and give you the full expansive understandings you now hold. And so move this day, knowing that each thing is as it needs to be with no regret, but perhaps looking upon each thing with a new awareness … with a new understanding, with Love and an embrace from Source Energy. For you see, Source Energy is an integral component and one that is most necessary. And it is the alignment with the one that will facilitate all you seek. It is in this way that you have found the keys to release any constraints and limitations that you may find yourself imposed upon, and imposed in, and imposed with at this point in time.

And so move this day. Move this day in a purposeful way so that you might embrace the more which is to be given. The more which is always available and which you will open up to as you move beyond these pages and these words that are so given in Love.

Recognize that all of life is a play. All of life is a play that is to be enjoyed and recognized, allowing, shifting, and moving you along the path — a most purposeful path. A path that you perhaps are aligning to now know. And do not make the query difficult. Do not allow the mind to circumnavigate and say how this must be so complicated that it cannot be deciphered or understood. For we will tell you this and that, and that and this are pure folly.

They are pure folly in that the understandings are more simplistic than you may recognize or be willing to see. And it is in the simplicity and the wonderment of the simplicity that you might now embrace. Embrace that which is easily ascertained. It is not a difficult measure. But the mind seeks to relate to you that it is most difficult. And how can you ever find this thing? For it is, and has, remained hidden for a time, and more time. And so, it must be difficult if you have not been able to ascertain it before.

But we would ask, has it been your number one priority at all times for a time? And if it has not, there is no worry that it has not, but now shift and move it to be the number one objective of the day, of the week, or perhaps longer. But move it into central focus so that it is unyielding from your gaze and view. Do not limit what you think upon it. Do not limit your day so that each day you return to wondering and musing upon this thing. Recognize its unparalleled importance — its significance. And the value that this knowingness would bring to you if you were to step into the portal of understanding what it is.

We will say most likely you will have not only done it within this time, but you have done an aspect of it in another time. But perhaps not given the full reckoning of what it is and the significance along with the awareness of what you are doing and now why you are doing it. For it is the completion. It is the returning of the 360 back to you in the full awareness of what you are now engaged in and upon.

Do you see the value here? Do you see the value of recognizing that you are completing what you set out to understand? And it is in this understanding … it is in this way … it is in this undertaking that you then engage life from a more profound and resounding way.

And so, we seek your engagement now as we move into another understanding that we wish to share at this time. Recognize that all beings on Earth are not of this understanding. That there are many that have come from other systems and worlds that sought a different experience and not the life purpose, and original purpose, and the purpose-driven objectives that you find yourself amidst and in.

And these beings share the land and the space in which you share. And they do move and look just like you. They are ingrained and allowed in this space where all are allowed in per the agreement. The agreement they work out and devise. So we will say that not all here are of this understanding and persuasion. We will say that all here are not as they appear to be. And so know that as you move and engage within your day, that each walking a path has a pathway that is unique and specific to them.

If you are reading this book and in search of your purpose, most likely it is something that applies to you. But we will say to resonate upon the words that are given, and when something does not align as it might not do, then you must sit with this to allow a bubbling up of recall to surface.

For you have been taught and ingrained with a certain understanding, or perhaps you have grown into an understanding, and now something that has been said is different than that. And you wonder — *How can that be? It does not seem right? It cannot be this way or that way. It must be the way that I knew before.* But might we suggest that you release your beliefs, for many times the mind does conjecture? The mind does wage a bit of war. The mind does seek to know all and is unwilling to yield the space in which you might grow to know more.

And so we would say to sit with it. Allow it to meld and move about you and allow the consideration of the words to infiltrate your psyche and being. And then sit with it some more. And then look again. Look again and ask within the heart space that you have now anchored, *what might be so?* Ask, and find what the answer provided might be as you release the expectation for the knowingness for which you hold now.

Might you consider this in the Loving embrace we now impart? For all life here is truly the mystery and the wonderment of the engagement, of the activity for the free will component that does exist … that does cause each to not truly know the path that will be taken at each moment of each day. There is a mystery, might we say, for you might choose this over that, and this step may move you closer, or that step may move you further away, but there is an engagement. There is an engagement of wonderment in all that does proceed as the free will component does become engaged. It does shift-change you to make this choice over that one … to go here rather than there. And to enlist the properties and the wonderment that does exist from one moment to the next by the choices made.

Will you embrace that and recognize that these choices allow you to traverse life on a different path than perhaps yesterday would have allowed or afforded. And we do not mean that in a negative way, but we mean that each day does have new opportunities that do grow and expand from each choice made. And the beauty and the wonderment of all that is, might be, is that which it is through the choices made and proffered within each and every day.

As life does move this day, know that all is a gift. Live life in the positive framework. Recognize that each pain, each ache, each body ailment might be looked upon also as a gift as you move to embrace that which is whole and healthy as you seek to recalibrate all that is in need of a boost.

Might we play a game now where you focus on one area that is needing just that boost? And as you focus there, feel its wholeness, feel the completeness of that area. And recognize that it is purposefully and fully aligned as it might be. And that as you add a component to the mix, you add Universal Love into all that is in, around, and through that area. See Universal Love swirling amidst and about the area in question. And now envision nothing but wholeness — nothing but health and vitality — nothing but completeness in what you are viewing now in the mind's eye as you visualize its restoration

and completeness as it moves in the full totality of all that it might be and more.

Will you focus upon this now for a few
moments, and then we will continue?

≈ Meditational Pause ≈

Might we now bring forward something in
a magical way into your being and world and
into your existence from this point moving
forward? What might you seek to know that
will allow you to manifest all that your heart
does desire and all that you have set into
motion to move into reality, into being in the
space that you now reside? What might that
be? And as you have stilled the mind, have
moved it away and from distraction, might
you once again focus on your heart center?

Might you focus there for a time?

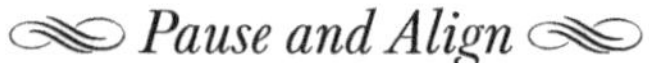

Pause and Align

As we proceed, know that Light and Love is a gift. It is a precious gift that you can emblazon, and embolden, and express within your day when you seek to do so, do you see? And so, recognize all within life is a choice. All within life is a choice that you elect to move forward or not. That you take strides to move into the pathway of purpose and to enact but do not meander or act in a laissez-faire way that you expect it to somehow be made manifest, and you wait impatiently for that thing to become known without putting in the work to have it occur.

And do you see that when you do not make it your number one priority, it will sit in limbo, so to speak? It will sit and not advance as you might prefer it to be. And then you, in an almost insistent sort of way, wonder why it is not here … why it has not become known. Why it is not in the full expanse of what it might be otherwise.

And it is in your degree of focus, intent, and purposeful desire to bring it into manifestation. And do you see if you do not do it, who else will be the one? You cannot enlist another to do your bidding in this way. For this is your undertaking, this was your Agreement; this was your intentful desire to know this thing above *all else*. And until you rise to the occasion, then the *all else* will not be … do you see?

And so remove distraction. Remove those things that do not need to be accomplished, except mentally. Do not do those things that pacify your mind. For in the pacification of the mind, and the pacification of the allowing of the mind to let you move this way or that, seek to regain that control.

Seek to regain that which is the most important thing that you have going on right now. Recognize it supersedes most everything. And we do not mean to distract you from those obligations with family and in other internal or outer doings. But we would say that this must become the priority. This must become the allness of being and the reason that you acknowledge why you are here.

For when you move in this way, when you move in the way of knowing that you are on the precipice of such a great discovery, then you will move in an unparalleled way. You will move in an unstoppable way. You will move in a way that you perhaps have not moved before.

For it is in the knowing, and the doing, and the being that this Agreement *will be no more.* You will have broken, let us say, the contractual obligation that was before you once before. And the Agreement will dissolve, for you will have reached the attainment of that which you desire.

And so move in this way this day. Move in the way of the breaking of that which is in many ways the tethering aspect that keeps you in this form, or that form, or another — until the discovery of what you set into motion has been found. And might you move with the expeditious and the all-encompassing way that this discovery will allow you to find.

And so we say, this is the offering that we give you. This is the opportunity to move forward in an unparalleled way when you connect within, still the mind, regain control, and move in that conscious way, in present moment awareness, positive thinking, and all that enacts these steps to be made manifest.

We give you our Light and Love if you will but call it into your being and world. We give you that which you desire and that which you intently and purposefully request so that you might move mountains, manifest the reality of your dreams, and bring all into fruition in this lifetime, now that you know more.

And might we say a bit more, for there is much more that is and will be known by you in time ...

About the Elders

Think upon Us as a Consciousness of Light and Love. Think upon Us as ever-moving light that does fluctuate and form words within the in-breath and out-breath of a beat or measure. Think upon Us as Love, in Love with all that is. We are Beings that wish for humanity to have answers that have eluded them in recent times. There are those who have shared such information, but it is also being released in this manner, in this time, so there might be a profound knowingness as one engages with life here. We are Pure Consciousness. We are many, and We provide insights for humanity so that more might be gleaned in this lifetime than without such knowledge. We are Love, but all are that which is.

About the Author

Robyn G. Locke bridges the physical with the nonphysical world to bring you their purpose-driven, self-healing, self-help books. She is a transformation facilitator, gifted speaker, energy intuitive, and spiritual seeker. *Love life and even what appears to be bad. Discover the deeper meaning attached to each thing encountered along the way. Engage in life's mystery.*

Her inspirational writings are given by the Elders. They provide invaluable insights and suggest refreshingly simple steps to engage. Imagine your future when mental constructs are removed and replaced with purposeful direction. Unbounded opportunities await as you consciously co-create all you desire to manifest.

Discover more at
www.AdvancedEnergetics.org

Find Our Books

Awaken
The Definitive Guide to Transformative Change

Do you have trouble manifesting what you want in life? Discover how to align your being and tap into those unlimited possibilities.

Feel like you're off-course? Hurdles stopping you in your tracks? Searching for guidance that seems no where to be found? Gifted speaker, change facilitator, and energy intuitive Robyn G. Locke conveys wisdoms given by the Elders – Beings of Pure Consciousness and Infinite Awareness. And now she's here to share powerful Universal insights to spark the means to enact a personal renewal of ultimate self-discovery.

Awaken: The Definitive Guide to Transformative Change is the must-have handbook for seekers desiring to co-create their best life. Its many exercises, relatable stories, meditational offerings, and other insightful approaches will help you release undesired negative energy and overcome those seemingly ever-present obstacles. Utilize new understandings and their platforms of possibility and promise as you relinquish self-limiting beliefs and discover new vistas.

In *Awaken*, you'll discover:

- How to easily, personally, and more readily transform your existence into one that manifests your dreams and desires
- Ways to unlayer and remove trapped emotional energy to help you shift-change into all you might be
- Instruction on the importance of your purpose and how you can step into this new pathway with confidence and ease
- Techniques that will self-heal, create wellness, and lead you to a more lasting happiness
- The ability to access inner fulfillment, shift-change your energy, see this life differently, and so much more

Awaken is an extraordinary resource accelerating the process of true inner awareness, restorative healing, and personal transformation. If you like enacting inspirational insights, garnering a deeper understanding of Universal Love's vast capabilities and timeless teachings, then get ready for the soul-stirring results these new discoveries will bring.

Are you ready to transform into more than your mind can currently fathom?

BOOK ONE

The Little Book to Find Your Purpose
WHEN ALL ALIGNS FOR YOU

What's the point without purpose? Do you seek inner fulfillment and yearn to discover more? Perhaps now is the time to:

- Learn more about the energy you are meant to enact and manifest here
- Discover the true value of Universal Love and how it can magically transform your life
- Recognize the significance of free will and why it's important to feel each experience created
- Understand how thoughts create feelings, and feelings create emotions bringing forth actions or reactions which result in your manifested reality
- Take steps to still and slow the mind; you are not your thoughts
- Produce better days when enlisting positive thoughts to replace those that don't feel good
- Release limitations and the negative what ifs of life as you engage in the positivity of what is now in play
- Find your roadmap to success, good health, and happiness as you consciously co-create all you desire and so much more

This *Little Book* provides fundamental and foundational knowledge for your platform of understanding. Universal Love is more keenly described so that you might move it into use today. Assimilate its intrinsic components, the means to still the mind, and the significance of your emotions.

BOOK TWO

The Original Purpose
ANSWERS THE AGE-OLD QUESTION — *Why Am I Here?*

Perhaps you've heard about it, but you haven't quite connected to what your purpose is. Maybe you're already enacting your life purpose but what about this original one? So if you've found your mission in this life, do you feel complete, fulfilled, or whole? Might you find your answers when you locate the original one? Discover your original purpose, find the gift in each adversity, and enlist change as you:

- Answer the age-old question, Why am I here?
- Reclaim your life, gain self-awareness, to become self-fulfilled
- Discover why asking questions, and more questions in the in-between time, is vital and key
- Connect to what you are meant to remember during your journey here
- Seek to get about implementing your purpose in a more expansive way
- Embrace change and some foundational truths as your trusted friend
- Employ steps to end the endless mental chatter
- Take steps to recognize and enact your original purpose as you seek to discover more

Step into a greater awareness as you move away from the proclivities of a mental knowingness that brought you adjacent to where you sought to be. Allow new insights to guide you back on course. Access what has been about you and within arms reach all along. Find those things that were always accessible yet had remained unknown.

Connect with Us

Find us at

www.AdvancedEnergetics.org

Facebook: @AdvancedEnergetics

Instagram: @AdvancedEnergetics

Twitter: @theEldersListen

YouTube: AdvancedEnergetics

* 9 7 9 8 9 8 7 7 5 4 2 8 3 *